X-Rated

Poems by

Larry Potash

L&M PRESS

The front cover illustration is a half tone of Eduoard Manet's "Dejuner sur L' Herbe" (Luncheon on the Grass). Through the selection of subject, realistic treatment, and coloration used in this painting, Manet repudiated the art of his day. As for the spotted dog in the half tone, it wandered into the scene quite by accident. It's significance, if any, remains unknown. The back cover illustration is taken from Pieter Bruegel's "The Fall of the Rebel Angels." It depicts a loyal angel, robed in light, sundering the defeated insurgents, gruesomely dark. Is this a metaphor for the fate of those who refuse to conform, who dare to dissent; or conversely, does it simply depict a civic poet hacking away at the legions of literary darkness?

ISBN: 0-9638688-0-2

CONTENTS

Illustrations

INTRODUCTION

One day in 1988 I received a phone call from Larry Potash. He had read my poetry in the **San Fernando Poetry Journal** where he had also been published and wanted to meet me and talk. From that simple beginning our friendship grew. We have long since recognized the similarities of our "outsider" role in the world of published writers and poets. Larry had articulated his kind of poetry as "Civic poetry; I had been content with simply writing mine as a voice from the outside. I have since adopted the "Civic Poet" designation for myself. It is a bit warmer within a descriptive category, not comfortable, but warmer.

The writing of poetry is complex. In bringing his words together, the poet makes great demands on his readers; the first responsibility, however, lies with the poet. What to write about? Are our times in need of "June, spoon, moon"? What times in history ever were? Potash, the civic poet, knows the standard arguments in academia over phanapoeta, mebpoeta or logpoeta, but he does not allow these viewpoints to interfere or disrupt his concerns over the human condition as we move towards the twenty-first century.

X-Rated is filled with protest and indignation, but Larry's magic manages to give us that occasional smile that we all can use. The humor in "By Way of Introduction", where we find that our "elephantine republic" has both a loaded rear and "lovely ivories", is elegant. The irony in Larry's short forceful poem "In The Asylum" describes the problem that a civic poet faces. He must comment on the world about him even though he knows full well that "no one is listening - nor apprehending". What words can best define the Civic Poet? Compassion mixed with anger; a strict sense of justice, not mere law, but justice. Law and justice are no longer one and the same (if they ever were); our litigious society has seen to that. Someone must stand up to a media that has created a society that voted for a Ronald Reagan, not once, but twice!

Larry and those few others that give of their time and talent in order to keep us aware of our responsibilities to the planet and to our humanity are today faced with a more difficult task than Thomas Paine. He faced a foe that lacked the contemporary exploiter's ability to mesmerize with dis- and misinformation. The civic poet's role is one of the powerless in defense of the powerless, and money has no place in this picture.

Would you like a clear view of the American political scene? Turn to "Frankie Goes To Washington" where the Baron "willed him a simple and beguiling smile" before he flew his creation Frankie Stein "to an artless culture, to America to make his fortune." Use your own imagination then; join the Baron in his lament over a "future president."

In "Dick and Jane" our "bare-knuckles poet" succeeds in creating an expose of our society in just 129 words, a remarkable display of his powers of observation and ability as a writer. For 'Melting Pot' dreamers, Larry gives us "Larry"s Dream". Are we a classless, color blind society?

Writers and the myriad number of 'safe' publishers, not to mention America's poets who should know better, are brought to account in "X-Rated" ("America's 'political' poets/ sedate us with general audience verse/ or inoffensively tantalize with literary soft porn/ that struts the barest bit of frontal nudity"). "X- Rated", "Shakespeare was a Nazi", and "Safe Poet" are three of Larry's poems that cry out against the silent and effective censorship that exists in our America.

Must we give Larry a political square to fit into? If I must, I do so only because there are no contemporary stables into which he can be boxed. Marxist? Capitalist? Socialist? Political Christian? None of these. All three econo-political systems have failed to provide an answer better than, "This is the least worst of all the systems." Larry will not settle for such a harebrained philosophy. He does however express the best of Jeffersonian ideals. He does not preach from any Biblical text and is certainly not 'respectful' enough to be a part of the great Christian brainwashed "Moral Majority". Pay close attention to his biting wit and strength in "They Say That They're Good Christians".

There are no signs of preachment in **X - Rated,** but Larry the Civic Poet does attempt to inform, to teach.

Does one teach if there is no hope for a better tomorrow?

The powerful screaming nightmare found in "Global Warning" was composed by Marilyn Potash and serves as a cautionary piece to punctuate the concerns over the human condition expressed by our poet. Concerns above and beyond academia's witless devotion to structure, form or rhyme that, like William H. Buckley, disregards the problems of the citizen.

Potash is a poet for our times. In "A Monorail Tour of the USA" Larry has somehow written a brief poem that summarizes the America of our day and it's prevailing philosophy, "Big Fish Eat Little Fish".

Reading about Schwarzkopf in "A Star Is Born", "Well now you're a household word commanding forty grand - maybe more - for each glowing speech" and then the poem "We Mop and Scour Floors" can be a humbling experience. In one, the two aspects of our society, the used and the users, are presented in stark relief. The other is an examination of life itself.

Potash closes this excellent collection of Civic Poetry with the poem "Artwork," leaving us something with which to remember him, something with which to thank him and those too few poets, writers and publishers who being artists "could not have done less."

PROFESSOR SALVATORE GALIOTO
September, 1993

ACKNOWLEDGEMENTS

I thank my wife, Marilyn, for her constant encouragement and patience without which I might not have published this book; for her artistic advice and editorial assistance; and for contributing the ecological poem, "Global Warning."

Thanks to the editors of the San Fernando Poetry Journal (Richard Cloke, Lori C. Smith, and Shirley Rodecker) who were willing to publish my more controversial poetry when I was wandering the literary wilderness. And thank you for continuing to do so. Similarly, my sincere thanks to the Editors of LaZer (Sarge Sterling, Ram Bhutani, Dennis McGinnis, Richard Pryor, and Syd Bradford) for publishing poetry that I thought would never see the light of day.

Finally, I thank Salvatore Galioto for first asking "Why don't you publish?", for his comments regarding the manuscript, and for his superb introduction.

Big Fish Eat Little Fish, after Pieter Bruegel

A Monorail Tour of the USA

Some say Theme Park USA's
an international tourist trap
but even they agree
its monorail imparts
an impelling sense of America.
Starting with a Yankee seaport town -
mm, smell the brine! -
the cars skim through rippling fields of wheat,
up and over the towering Rockies -
get that whiff of pine! -
across the Great Salt Lake,
by western prairie herds,
past gambling casinos in Nevada
and the snowy ski-slopes of Tahoe,
down California's central valley,
and then, as oxygen masks descend,
draw up to a sprawling metropolis
enveloped by a pall of smog.
On this city's border
affluent walled suburbs appear;
then suddenly, as the train veers
toward the poorer inner core,
it banks steeply to avoid indiscriminate fire
from brawling gangs and dueling drug lords.
Slowly, the cars crawl past burnt out blocks
ransacked in the last riot;
then, while the train creeps over encampments
of imploring urban poor,

the passengers drag out bags
of tour bought edibles and small change
and soon candy, stale rolls, and quarters
rain down on USA's shabbier residents.
And now the well-off travelers smile
at our entrepreneurial style
of social problem solving
as they read the sign,
"Welcome to LA,
   it's the end of the line."

By Way of Introduction

I have a cousin
that stands by this elephant
called America.
On the forefront,
she's oriented for the ivories
and to tender her honest tribute
she should stand at the head
of her elephantine republic
but by diligently bringing up the rear
perhaps I merit a place also
for someone should impartially deride
its unpalatable side -
that in addition to lovely ivories
there's a hell of a lot of shit.

May He Sleep in Peace

Would you believe
I had a grandfather
was so grateful
for his second start
in the new land
he turned tax refunds
back to Uncle Sam
sayin, "keep it, it pleases me"
- may he sleep in peace.
Now his niece
fudges on taxes
howsoever she can
and the favorite grandson
writes verse satire
panning
mean ole Uncle Sam.

Ode to Sid and Johnny

Sid Vicious and Johnny Rotten,*
troubadours for disaffected youth
who crammed a rod of musical dynamite
up an impassive Britain's ass -
where are you now?!
Sid and Johnny,
in 90s' America
with it's metastatic inequality
and flagging economy,
we need your drumming wake-up calls,
your reviling Punk-art-terrorism,
for events are brewing
compared to which
your discordant notes
may sound positively sweet.

* Members of the pioneering Punk group, the "Sex Pistols."

"Repent!" Modified from drawing by Bruegel

In the Asylum

Like petulant blackbirds
cawing ill omens,
raucous poets declaim,
"Repent!"
though knowing them lunatic
no one is listening -
not apprehending
we're merely half crazy.

The City By the Sea

At first light
I dimly fathomed the city
hovering above a hazy sea
and in that city,
fashioned from the flotsam
of a thousand nations,
I conjured a favored folk,
flourishing and free.
Touring its teeming beach, one noon,
I glimpsed my city's battered poor.
And as succeeding immigrant waves
washed their casualties
from its littered shore
I pondered,
"What could cleanse the conscience
 of my city by the sea?"

City By the Sea

The Inheritance

In a trendy gallery,
as wealthy patrons drifted by,
I eyed a singular painting,
a Nativity presenting Madonna and child
nursing on a littered floor
attended by pigs and goats
and a trio of army brass
peering imperiously through the door.
Judging from their rural garb
and darkly glowing complexion,
mother and infant
could have been campesinos
from a dozen Latin nations -
though were setting and dress
a little different
Ethiopia, Bangladesh,
or even American poor
would have been equally plausible.
And mingled with the dirt,
beneath beamy Madonna's blackened feet,
her maker's caption asserted:
"Blessed are the meek
 for they shall inherit the earth."

They're Kind of Like Meatballs

They're kind of like meatballs.
Take rice, crackers, bread crumbs, or cornmeal;
mix in an egg (cooking oil will do);
shake on salt, pepper, a tad of other spices;
add a bit of diced celery or onion
and stir in some gravy or soy sauce.
Lastly shape and pan fry.
Now drown "meatballs" in diluted ketchup
or tomato paste
and spoon on pasta for a satisfying feast.
Finally, for that tasty, low calorie dessert,
mix jello with fruit, cookie crumbs, or some other sweet.
While actually this recipe's for dining on the cheap,
you may soon be devising similar dishes
and nowadays for millions of Americans
it's a far healthier, more welcome diet
than they normally have to eat.

Their Bus Never Comes*

Waiting for a bus that never comes,
almost 400 homeless sleep on wooden benches
and toilet seats
in San Francisco's Transbay Terminal.
Too soon their refuge will close at night
and these outcasts will be found
dozing at another site,
possibly the streets.
But for those skeptics who object
this sketch suggests a scene from India,
knowledgeable observers point out
that in Calcutta
the benches are wider.

* Based on a San Francisco Chronicle article published
  July 23, 1993

People Got to Eat

People Got to Eat
else you mean, cravin
achin bout the belly;
all i know
People Got to Eat,
gotta work to eat
so here's the point,
the tightening circle,
People Got to Eat,
You cut us small
cause we outta work
now we dressin you,
yah got no jobs,
you ain't worth a damn!

The Last American Factory Worker

That's our last American factory worker
hanging on my wall,
a PR crew shot his hopeful photo
before we relocated in Mexico.
Now notice how he smiles and waves
as his plant's final auto rolls by the gate.
Earlier, when we lobbied for tax relief
and his representatives so greedily complied
not caring if we transferred to Mexico
as long as they got their bribe,
that fellow hurrahed and waved our corporate flag.
He was, how may I say it, so easily gratified.
And when employee benefits stayed conspicuously costly
and America's payrolls comparatively high,
I sent my memos; soon all production ceased...
Now come, we'll tour our maquiladora.
Doubtless, you'll agree, it's the finest in our industry...
Of course, someday, I'll visit you;
then we'll see about a factory in Peru.
Oh, him? His family? Truly, I don't know...
Though why should anyone care?
We laid him off six years ago...

Frankie Goes to Washington*

The town plaza filling, clamorous burghers were milling,
not by cudgel or firebrand committed
but fitted with flashlight, faith, and fair intention
when the originator, their mad instigator,
the infamous baron intoned,
"Affrighted villagers and neighbors
 from choicest cadavers
 to foster science and humankind
 I sutured my monster, Frankie Stein,
 and, to assure my dominion, willed him simple
 and a beguiling smile crafted for his safety
 then flew him to an artless culture,
 to America to make his fortune.
 Unexpectedly, by midlife he aged radical
 and in his wake American social progress lies gutted,
 seven ghettoes have been razed,
 ten thousand paupers moulder disemboweled."
At which the mayor lamented,
"A rampaging radical's disquieting
 he must be extraordinarily revolting."
"An ultraconservative," the baron declared.
"Then he's all right," the mayor consoled.
"So unconscionably successful," the baron confided,
"he's elected to audition for his greatest role
 Frankie Stein for president,
 and with his captivating smile
 I'm afraid he'll fill top billing."
"Then our problem's simple," a labor leader called,
"on this bad actor we'll run an expose
 and ring a curtain call."
"Americans are an abiding nation," the baron cautioned,
"Let a candidate command a smile
 and they'll glibly gambol on Armageddon

disparaging imprudent critics as unkind."
Then a clergyman proposed,
"Perhaps through patience and understanding
 we might teach him to be truly caring,
 that the human race is the only race worth winning."
"He's uneducable," the baron replied,
 the single thing he's learned is when to smile."
The clergyman sputtered, "Then somewhere
 stalking their inmost fears
 slinking down American streets
 impervious to blandishment or reason
 haunts our creation, a future president."
"And may God have mercy on us all," the baron cried.

Dancing in the Streets*

"Nigger! Down on the concrete!
Yeah you! Move! Fuckin Move!"

Man, it's like Vietnam,
there's a war goin on,
a war goin on!
An we're battling in the streets,
battling in the streets!
Cause it's open season
on slum city niggers,
on young an bum city niggers.
Hear the sirens an the beatings,
the sirens an the beatings,
as no hope cuts us down
as dope cuts us down,
as...

Hey mad fool, all you hear's cool
black rhythm n' blues;
an we're jus dancin in the streets
to the inner city beat,
the inner city beat.

* "...young black teenagers are reported to be the
oldest and the newest creatures added to the
endangered species list. As of now the
government has not taken steps to preserve the
blacks...," lines from music recorded by the rap
singer 'Ice Cube.'

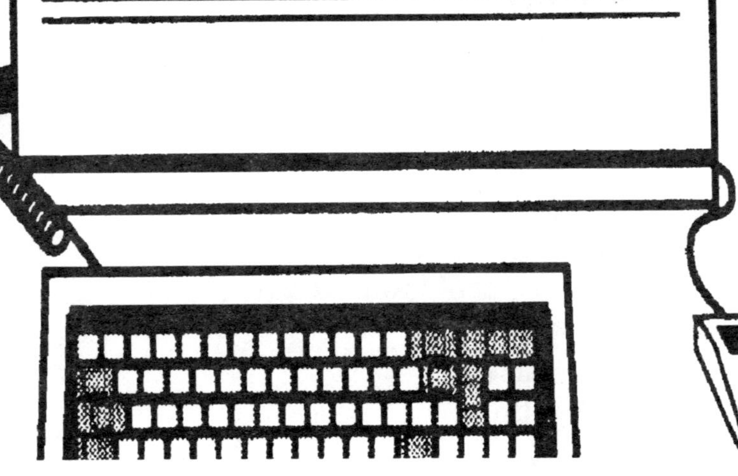

Hidden Characters

When words frolic capriciously
on my monitor
one menu option lets me see
space markers, carriage returns,
and other normally invisible characters
configuring my lines.
Now wouldn't it be prudent
if society's more affluent kinds
commissioned an equivalent selection
to discover their hidden figures
(assembly-line workers, file clerks,
word processors, paramedics,
waiters, telephone operators ...)
for if these stalwarts stay unseen
everyone could find
things don't work for anyone!

Dick and Jane

From middle class sired,
fabulous Dick and Jane
blossomed
in that inherited adulation
of police, their postman,
pliant Spot,
and a grateful nation.
Surmounting adolescence,
Jane sauntered on to college,
married by 22,
worked at marketing,
labored 1.5 kids,
though undeniable privation,
not one immaculate orgasm.
Liberated lately,
and importuning Johns,
that doyenne of vaginal pathos
proselytizes in bars,
mulling why in hell
she merely whets imperfection.
Dick, unalloyed,
deployed at graduation
by General Dynamics,
sported in Sunnyland,
where cavorting about waterbeds,
snorting coke,
he O.D.'d on America,
bought a Bugatti,

registered Republican,
and tooled on into the sunset
of the great American dream.
Now, draped in cardigan,
mien and ivory grin,
on semen nights
he cruises by
Merica n' Vine
acculturating comely kids
to hop in awhile
and spin.

Hannibal the Cannibal

Hannibal the Cannibal,
when movie goers watched you
in "Silence of the Lambs"
many thought they saw
a serious social imperfection,
after all, eating people raw
is quite an unappetizing oddity,
(even worse than biting nails
or picking boogies from one's nose.)
Those viewers simply didn't realize
that your biggest personal flaw
was merely that you thought too small.
If only you'd acted on a grander scale,
become an overachiever
like a Hitler, a Pol Pot, an Idi Amin,
or even a Milosevic,
you might have been
a revered national leader,
a world-class political player,
a feted international darling.
But then, I suppose,
not everyone's destined
for the "Paths of Glory."

Hang Ups

Claudius*,
by mild palsy favored,
feigned the fool
and so, beguiling many,
bided a respectable span
to be hung with royal purple,
lauded emperor of Rome.
Applauded by few,
Christ featured himself
"son of God"
and so enjoyed
his somewhat shorter run,
the crowning role,
a Judean felon
hung up on a cross.

* Tiberius Claudius Drusus Nero Germanicus
  (e.g. Claudius I) 10 B.C. - A.D. 54

"In God We Trust." I thank Edvard Munch
and William Blake for their contributions.

"In God We Trust"

Now all right God,
when Stalin liquidated twenty million,
give or take a few,
sweety and I paid no notice,
we still believed in You.
And even after Hitler'd gassed six million
we simply said,
"Hey, He's got other things to do."
And later, as the Khmer Rouge
snuffed out an erring million or two,
still, we believed in You.
Then only yesterday, while Muslim, Croat, Serb
impassively slayed each other,
we didn't even waver;
yes, we believed in You.
Yet now, on this very day, dear Lord,
my loving mate lies dying.
And we've got to set things straight.
You've let things get out of hand;
You're truly trying credibility.
So come on God!
Isn't there anything you can do?!

They're Serving You

Here's a prime house recipe
from governance and advertising
for dispensing sizzle instead of steak:

- Take a slice of nothing
- Garnish with mouth watering terms
- Serve piping patriotically
- Retain sycophants who'll certify your beef!

Yet don't stew. Dedicated to you,
they're presently cooking up
that internationally publicized special,
"freedom of speech,"
a platter of democratic ham
liberally stuffed with baloney.
And anybody who'll swallow that
doesn't go hungry!

Talking Heads

This illuminating exchange was secretly recorded
at the home of a well-to-do Wall Street broker
where politicians, lobbyists, and campaign contributors
had congregated to choose a presidential candidate:

Noted the broker, "Past experience shows
  we need a nominee who hasn't entertained
  a controversial thought or deed..."
"Then," quipped a contributor,
"Why not dig up someone who's dead?"
"But yet," counseled another,
"though tranquilly reposing,
  a corpse might previously have acted imperfectly
  so let's resurrect someone that succumbed in infancy
  and, after programming a telegenic persona,
  hire add agencies and endow think tanks
  to concoct a congenial personal history
  and then tape thirty second spots for TV."
 The broker-host responded, "There's much to be said
  for computer generated imagery
  and, as modern presidents are chiefly actors,
  clearly, our most promising candidate
  is the one who's best at delivering another's lines."
"But," interjected a politician skeptically,
"Surely an opposing party
  would pull the plug on such a bogus operation!"

**Slyly, the broker smiled,
"As our two major parties
 play on the same corporate team
 we'll ask a common sponsor
 to induce the other party
 to run a similarly programmed candidate -
 then who'll be the wiser?"**

Although you may demur
this transcription's a preposterous parody
and that your cherished candidate's persona
isn't simply programmed by the highest bidder,
when you switch on your TV
look and listen more carefully.
Could a mere person smile and lie with such perfection?!

Don't Bite the Hand

Although authorities teach,
"Don't bite the hand that feeds you,"
isn't it simply sensible to crunch down hard
if you're being handed shit?!

A Doctor Speaks*

America, as I'm a civic practitioner
who won't let an affliction pass,
I'll verse what my literary peers
don't dare jot a solitary line of;
mainly, you're languishing with anal occlusion,
or, to diagnose your malaise clearly,
America, you've got a plug up your ass.
But I'll communicate more curatively:
My ideologically impacted nation
why not actually be
that bountiful, beautiful home of the free
(which is healthier for yourself, the world,
and, not to mention, artists such as me?)

* "It is by the grace of God that in our country we have
   those three unspeakably precious things: freedom of
   speech. freedom of conscience, and the prudence
   never to practice either of them," Mark Twain

American Happiness

America's preponderant whites
maintain that true happiness,
like Jesus, must be white.
Afro-Americans know that prospects
for an American happiness
are actually black;
while minority Asians
especially favor
Chinese, Vietnamese, or Korean shadings.
These days, gays of varied races
say personal happiness is truly being gay;
yet, unruly radicals protest
that their best happiness
is being in some other place.

Downward Mobility

Life's one dismal ache,
by no fault of my own
a hope strewn seismic zone
after a 6.5 quake
on the cultural Richter scale.
Apparently, my incautious patter
rattled America's upper strata.
Pacific plates grumbled;
adamant mountains shuddered;
shaken volcanoes flipped their lids;
though oddly, even as I stumbled
head over heels into the widening abyss,
I took comfort that my fall was free.

Tomorrow He May Be*

After Stalin's cultural hack, Zhdanov,
had treated the major Soviet poet, Akhmatova,
to yet another round of denunciation,
at a select soiree, Akhmatova turned to a tested friend
and through tears brought by too much laughter,
whispered, "Today, Zhdanov is my oppressor,
 tomorrow... tomorrow he may be
 a footnote to my poetry."

* In September 1946 both Akhmatova and Zoshchenko
 were expelled from the Union of Writers. In October
 1988, under "glasnost", the expulsion was rescinded.

The Poets' Union

Maybe what we writers need
is a poets' union,
then TV's newspersons might recite,
"Poets declare strike.
 Tomorrow, there'll be no poetry in America."
Come to think of it,
knowing the poetry of the past ten years,
maybe American poets *are* on strike
and perhaps TV's commentators should shout,
"Come on poets
 let's go back to work!"

Modified from IWW Poster,   "I Will Win"

Amiri's "Black Art"

LeRoi Jones or Amiri Baraka
as you will
you were right, we need poems that kill
and love,
have an orgasm
or take a crap,
poems to piss on poets
who're mongering art.*
Blunt as death,
tender as a bayonet,
Amiri
versed with showing heart.

* "What do you think an artist is? An imbecile who has only
his eyes if he's a painter, or ears if he's a musician, or a lyre
at every level of his heart if he's a poet...? On the contrary,
he's at the same time a political being, constantly alive
to heartrending, fiery or happy events to which he responds
in every way... No, painting is not done to decorate apartments.
It is an instrument of war for attack and defense against
the enemy [the person who exploits others]." Pablo Picasso

Lady with a hat, after Kirchner

X-Rated

Purveying fashionable platitudes,
America's "political" poets
sedate us with general audience verse
or inoffensively tantalize with literary soft porn
that struts the barest bit of frontal nudity,
the occasional cultural thigh or tit
as with, " I'm against ecological disaster;"
or "the homeless shouldn't have to sleep on our streets,"
Now you may think such smut's explicitly sexual,
but as for me, I expect our political poetry
to probe society with a civic practitioner's proctoscope,
to graphically pose cultural pubic hair,
to factually show groaning, sweating, panting, moaning,
to incite a suppressed, impotent audience to get it off,
and oh yes - you've guessed it
- to expose "the naked truth."
And so I flaunt unadorned porn that glares
you are America's chief social disease
- no condoms, please!
that you're more hazardous than any nuclear bomb,
that in America "freedom of speech"
is more apparent than real,
that our media's vaunted objectivity is mostly lip service
- a cultural blow job,
that there's only one political party, the business party,
that your greed, your indifference
(and sometimes my own) is nauseating,
that...so okay, I'll take my mandatory X-rating proudly
and, at inception, loudly stamp it on every verse I write
- then, who knows,
maybe I'll attract more readers that way!

"Shakespeare was a Nazi," altered from title-page of First Folio

Shakespeare Was a Nazi

As soliciting with outrageous ease
our title struts the little hooker
jauntily flaunting her buns at honesty
why sanctimoniously suppose
authentic art never lies
rather than contemplate this more plausible fable?
Let's propose
prodigious Shakespeare's currently composing,
this author of such enormous talent
who could versify bloodletting
and not dribble lines of ketchup
but of real blood,
and craft him a political poet -
albeit an American one -
where would Shakespeare publish?
In high circulation magazines
that serve as havens
for unexceptional, noncontroversial art?
To form our answer plainly - Not a chance!
As he'd scandalize those subscribers
truly Christ couldn't publish there.
Then what about purely literary journals?
Would that mighty line
that could resonate like a plummeting fighter plane,
sound human depths with our finest literary sonar,
or gently stir a crowd
like the current desire for nuclear disarmament,
grace those esoteric pages?

Surprisingly seldom as their literary auditors assume
Social Concern and that consummate virgin, Art,
couldn't advantageously cohabit,
that the principal issue's a craftless bastard.
And so belatedly, if he didn't eschew poetry,
the surpassing Shakespeare would inadvertently become
a bard of computer bulletin boards
and specialized little presses
which sanction deliberation
of moral/political alternatives -
our American samizdat.

Safe Poet

Of purest social conscience
Safe Poet exudes sure literary taste;
now note how his avid audience gazes
at that impeccably consonant face.
Soon they'll repose tranquilly, grazing
on his latest civil art*
without a solitary spur of locoweed
to profane their pasturage.

* "Art does not render the visible; rather, it makes visible."
  Paul Klee

"Freedom of the Press," after drawing by Art Young

Our Democratic License

Subdued solely by consuming preference
and insufficient creativity
a litany of upstanding genitalia
solicits marketplace exposure.
Censor a single prurient vision
one lascivious phrase
and the consequence is revocation
of our democratic license
but as capitalism's our profession
we couldn't commend liberty
that confuses brand recognition
like displaying socialism on TV;
besides, our commercial grasp of history
profiting on millennia of franchising campaigns
manufactures two political goods,
Republican and Democrat;
consequently, any premise or promise
not the stock option of enterprising candidates
is not worth advertising anyway.

Capitalist Realism

Once upon a writer's congress
a Marxist despot and his literary lackeys
acclaimed a dictum called socialist realism
that commanded Soviet literature be
an historically authentic depiction
of communist ascension to a worker's paradise.
Accordingly, in occasionally literate,
sometimes animated prose,
tomes were penned extolling proletarian heroes
and their utopian socialist nation
where blemishes such as gulags, famines, show trials,
rationally couldn't exist.
And so those engineers of the human spirit
promoted the Soviet genre of socialist uplift,
a literary heir to that idyllic fancy
where prancing rustics piped in sunlit fields
fleecing docile little white ewes.

Now hey down, woe down, golly way down,
we'll contrast America's current literary fare,
capitalist realism.
This exclusive fashion differs from the socialist genre
in that its impeccable persona
is the successful professional,
lawyer, stockbroker, physician, executive
- no worker heroes here!
And while our dissident or nonconforming author
is left to free market forces,

like book prohibition, lawsuit, and sponsor coercion,
an overweening paper and electronic media
eulogize the unrelenting, affluent achiever
their balmy moral beaming:
"Recession, poverty, homelessness notwithstanding
 when you're aiming high
 the sky's the limit!"
By contrast, America's rarely evident laboring castes
are scornfully caricatured as abject asses
(If they undeniably show intelligence and panache
why aren't they middle class?!)
Then hey down, woe down, golly way down;
lastly, we'll applaud those improbable intrigues
capitalist realism's practitioners weave.
For instance, could you believe
a glitzy, TV evangelist*
has a tryst with the church secretary
who hails from Babylon (New York)
and subsequently is brought to ruin,
while Miss Kiss N. Tell, explicitly baring all,
cohabits illicitly in a Playboy mansion
with America's soft porn king?
Oops! That's actually factual!
In the consuming spectacle signifying Americana
how inconsequential the solo author's imagination
when infinitely more implausible is daily actuality!

* Jim Baker of course!

Smiley Uncle Sam

An American Lullaby

On my bedroom wall
hangs a smiley Uncle Sam
with long striped pants an hat,
an a crinkly flag in hand.
An when I'm worryin
an can't sleep
cause I'm liable to lose my job
an be kicked out on the street,
I pray to kindly Uncle Sam
my soul to keep
an count America's blessins
instead a sheep.
Then beneath the snugly sheets
I fall to grinnin
an to feelin specially good,
an soon I'm fast asleep,
I'm fast asleep.

They Say That They're Good Christians

They say that they're good Christians -
I prefer the lions!
Good Christians
are saintly
self sacrificing
doers of good deeds.
Good Christians,
unlike unicorns and fair maidens,
are rarely to be found.
Lions value family life,
sport strong passions
and voracious appetites.
Lions are plain people
just like you and me.

Larry's dream

Like that prince of racial harmony,
Martin Luther King,
I had a dream the other night,
and in that incredible dream
women and men, Asian, black, Hispanic, and white,
were playing on an all-American team...

It was a summer scorcher
and the bottom of the ninth.
Our all-American pitcher,
straight, fair-haired, and blue eyed,
peered at the batter
then, after leering at her protuberant rear,
took a mighty wind-up
and fired the ball past the plate
where the latina-lesbian-American catcher
flipped him a bird
and made the umpire retrieve it.
On the third pitch
the batter popped a lazy fly
past the Korean-American first baseperson
who had it in her glove,
when she was felled
by the charging Afro-American right-fielder
yelling, "Who the hell let Koreans play?!"
So the hitter made it to first.
Then, after two strikes,
to catch the runner stealing to second,

the pitcher whipped the ball
to an alternatively-abled, triple-hyphenated,
second base person
who, having two left hands
and four right feet,
dropped the ball and missed his tag.
Nonetheless, the Euro-Hebraic-American umpire
ruled the runner out; for, as she smugly upheld,
"America need's an even playing field
  that levels everyone equal
  regardless of race, ethnicity, or ability."
Then the manager for the opposing team
stormed onto the field screaming,
"This is international competition!"
"We don't play by American rules!"
So grudgingly, the umpire relented
calling the player, "S A F E!"
Then the second batter sacrificed
leaving two out and a runner on third.
The next hitter slammed a searing grounder
which the shortstop fielded brilliantly
but being a white-fundamentalist-American-male
he couldn't bring himself to toss it
to the latina-lesbian-American catcher.
So the opposing team earned the winning run...

And all the while wildly cheering
though never wholly knowing the score
due to endless declarations of an extraordinary victory
for equal opportunity and personal liberty,
the stands thought team-America victorious.

American Pioneers Circa 1992

With winter's layoffs, as we'd both lost our jobs
an couldn't find no others,
we headed west.
Ben an me took the worst clunker
while Beth, my oldest,
drove behind with the boys in another.
An I'll tell you
we didn't mess with any of them fancy restaurants;
instead, we just nibbled on bread
an peanut butter an jelly,
an, oh yes, plenty a cookies.
An when we was sleepy -
cept for once, when my chest pains got so bad
we thought itid be better
if I rested in a real bed -
we napped in them drafty cars
in the damp March air.
Even so, the kids had a grand time!

Well, we made it!
An maybe, when Ben an me find us good jobs
with some medical insurance,
I'll see a doctor then.
Now, things'll surely go better.
They will - won't they?!

Marching! Marching!

1. Marching!

We're marching! Joyously marching,
jackboots tromping,
we're marching -
marching off to where?
Who cares?!
Note our jubilant tune!
For we're marching! Marching
to an hup! Two! Three!...
Everyone's marching, Marching!
For we've millennia to strut
and worlds to be won,
before our music's done,
before our music's done.

2. Marching!

"Whad are we fightin for?!"

It's hup! Two! Three! Four!
For we're marching! Joyously marching,
jackboots stomping,
we're marching -
"Marching off to where?"
"Who cares?!"

A Star Is Born*

General Schwarzkopf,
we all knew
you had it in you.
With a supporting cast of millions
(including Iraqi extras),
you took star billing.
Well, now you're a household word
commanding forty grand -
maybe more -
for each glowing speech.

*However, at times like Easter
we're reminded
that two millennia before
our secular days
a shepherding star
rose in the east
but unlike you,
forsaking other's easy lines,
Christ died crucified -
and poor!*

* "The Persian Gulf payoff may be only beginning
   for the generals who led U.S. forces to
   victory...General H. Norman   Schwarzkopf...
   could command seven figure [CEO] salaries,
   extraordinary speaker fees and sky's the limit
   spokesman incomes...," from an Associated Press
   Article published in March 1991.

I Hear a Symphony

When it seemed thematic
our president and his instrumentalists
drummed up a media fortissimo
for an antiseptic war
that could run five days,
maybe a month -
no more.
And such compelling orchestration!
But when discordant notes
flew trebling through the air
he and his accompanists
played at contrapuntal variation,

"As months or even longer
        It'll be an antiseptic war
abet the better tempo
        that'll last five days
give us a hand
        maybe a month -
for an expanded coda.
        no more."

Now maybe you applaud
well crafted polyphonics
but I've heard that score
too many times before -
I want a new arrangement 

Music to the Ears*

First there's the drum roll
splintered by a
BOOM!
Finally, an increasing whine
- terrifying -
then the thunderclap,
sometimes shrieks.
This time, a sigh of relief,
"Thank God! it hit
    someplace else!"

* Based on a newspaper report from Sarajevo

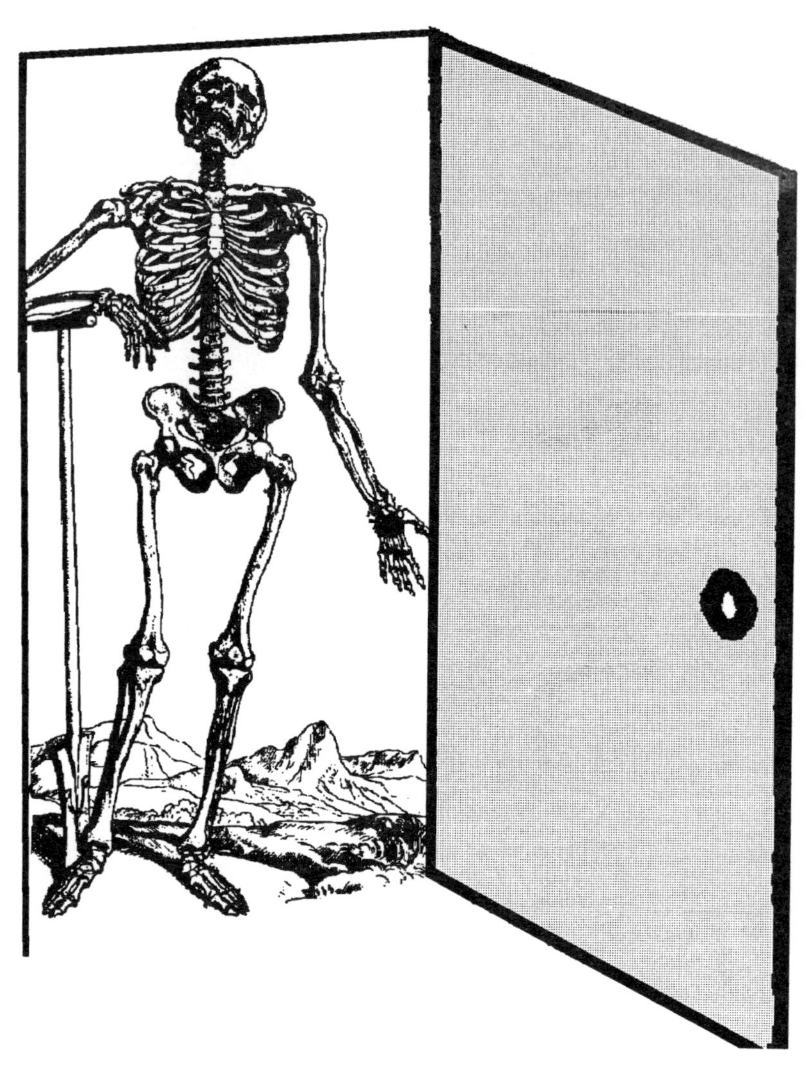

"A bleached Skeleton for a Man...By the Door,"
skeleton and outdoor background after Vesalius.

We Mop and Scour Floors

We mop and scour floors,
dust the tables and the drawers,
tidy journals and old magazines,
sweep the patio and railings,
clean as best we're able;
but as we're sipping ceremonial coffee
Entropy, who bided patiently at the table,
laughs to witness such hauteur,
folds her sleeves and goes to work.
Spiders decamping from odd corners
rappel down indiscernible cords,
dust swarms over spots of bright
drawn to antique furniture tops,
giggling kids track in off the street
stamping prints on the linoleum floor
while we helplessly implore,
"Wipe those feet!"
Remorselessly, a bleached skeleton for a man
garbed in black
grins eerily by the door.

Global Warning*

Leafless trees stand tall and terse
Upon the frozen, frigid earth.

No babbling brook breaks the stillness
Against this arctic wilderness.

No winter wind howls in the gray ghostly sky
Where just yesterday flocks of geese flew hurriedly by.

Now and then a synthetic sound shrieks
in these abysmal lands
Of phantom wolves that hungrily howl
in banished bands.

And no mortal creature crawls forth
from this endless dark dank ground;
Only empty stillness awaits
the tireless turning of time around.

* Poem contributed by Marilyn Potash

As a Scientist

As a scientist
I imagined it sublime
to play the poet;
now that I'm a poet
I suppose it's fine
to be a scientist.

Cast Aside My Poetry

Cast aside my poetry
as wine by inattention
a trifle bitter turned.
So futile
voguish art to imitate
with immortality illusory,
its' premises pat lies.
Poets write, bequeath our echoes,
and, like Christ,
are forgotten long ago.

Artwork

My life never was a work of art
nor ever have I mistaken art for life;
merely, I've endeavored to reach truthfully
with poetry the restricted syntax of my speech.
But then candidly, could I, an artist, have done less?
Judging by the tomes of others, evidently yes.